I0800021

TIMELINES IN SCIENCE

THE ELECTRIC AGE

Craig Boutland

ROSEN PUBLISHING

Published in 2025 by The Rosen Publishing Group, Inc.
2544 Clinton Street, Buffalo, NY 14224

Portions of this work were originally authored by Charlie Samuels and published as *The Advent of Electricity*. All new material in this edition was authored by Craig Boutland.

PICTURE CREDITS
t=top, b=bottom, l=left, r=right, c=center

Front Cover: Shutterstock: Billion Photos main, Ryan M Bolton tr, Cones tc, Yama Hilb tl.
Inside: Alamy: Science Photo Library 25, The Picture Art Collection 10; Library of Congress: 44, 54, 55; Look and Learn: 11, 13, 22, 42; NASA Images: JPL 12; Public Domain: 24, 45, courtesy AIP Emilio Segré Visual Archives Physics Today 56, Enricos 23, Geological Society, London/Sedwick Museum 7b, National Szechenyl Library/Agnes Szemeredi 43, Thinkstock/Photos.com 7t, 14, 15t&b, 18, 19, 26, 31, 39t&b, 40tr, 41, 50, 51, 60; Shutterstock: Awe Inspiring Images 59, James Cox 21t, Steven L. Hermann 29, Alexander Kaths 35, Sebastian Kaulitzki 5, Kateryna Larina 30, Mixrinho 57, Mikhail Pogosov, 34, Tatiana Popova 52t, Dr Morley Read 6, SciePro 38, Sportgraphic 47; Topfoto: 58, HIP 46, The Granger Collection 17.

All other artwork and illustrations Brown Bear Books Ltd

Cataloging-in-Publication Data

Names: Boutland, Craig.
Title: The electric age / Craig Boutland.
Description: Buffalo, NY : Rosen Young Adult, 2025. | Series: Timelines in science | Includes glossary and index.
Identifiers: ISBN 9781499477764 (pbk.) | ISBN 9781499477771 (library bound) | ISBN 9781499477788 (ebook)
Subjects: LCSH: Electricity–History–Juvenile literature. | Electricity–Juvenile literature. | Electricity–Experiments–History–19th century–Juvenile literature.
Classification: LCC
QC527.2 B68 2025 | DDC 537–dc23

Manufactured in the United States of America

CPSIA Compliance Information: Batch #CSRYA25.
For further information, contact Rosen Publishing at 1-800-237-9932.

CONTENTS

Introduction

The 19th century marked many scientific turning points. By its end, scientists had worked out the answers to problems that could still only be guessed at in 1800.

Where did humans come from? How did organisms inherit qualities from their parents? How old was Earth? What were the building blocks of substances? How did disease spread? And what was the nature of electricity? By 1900, researchers had come up with answers to such questions that are still largely accepted today. Many of the individual scientists were enthusiastic amateurs, as in earlier decades. By the end of the century, however, science was increasingly a specialized pursuit followed in laboratories by academics who were effectively professional scientists.

Theory and Practice

Many of the developments covered in this book were theoretical. People made careful observations and studies and then developed a theory to explain them. Charles Darwin's theory of evolution, Gregor Mendel's theory of genetics, and Dmitri Mendeleyev's theories about the nature of elements could only be proved later, when scientific knowledge caught up with their insights. Other developments were practical, however, and few were as influential as the invention of the internal combustion engine, which would begin a transportation revolution and lead to the coming of not only the age of the motor car but also of the airplane.

About This Book

This book uses timelines to describe scientific and technological advances from about 1800 to about 1900. A continuous timeline of the period runs along the bottom of all the pages. Its entries are color-coded to indicate the different fields of science to which they belong. Each chapter also has a subject-specific timeline, which runs vertically down the edge of the page.

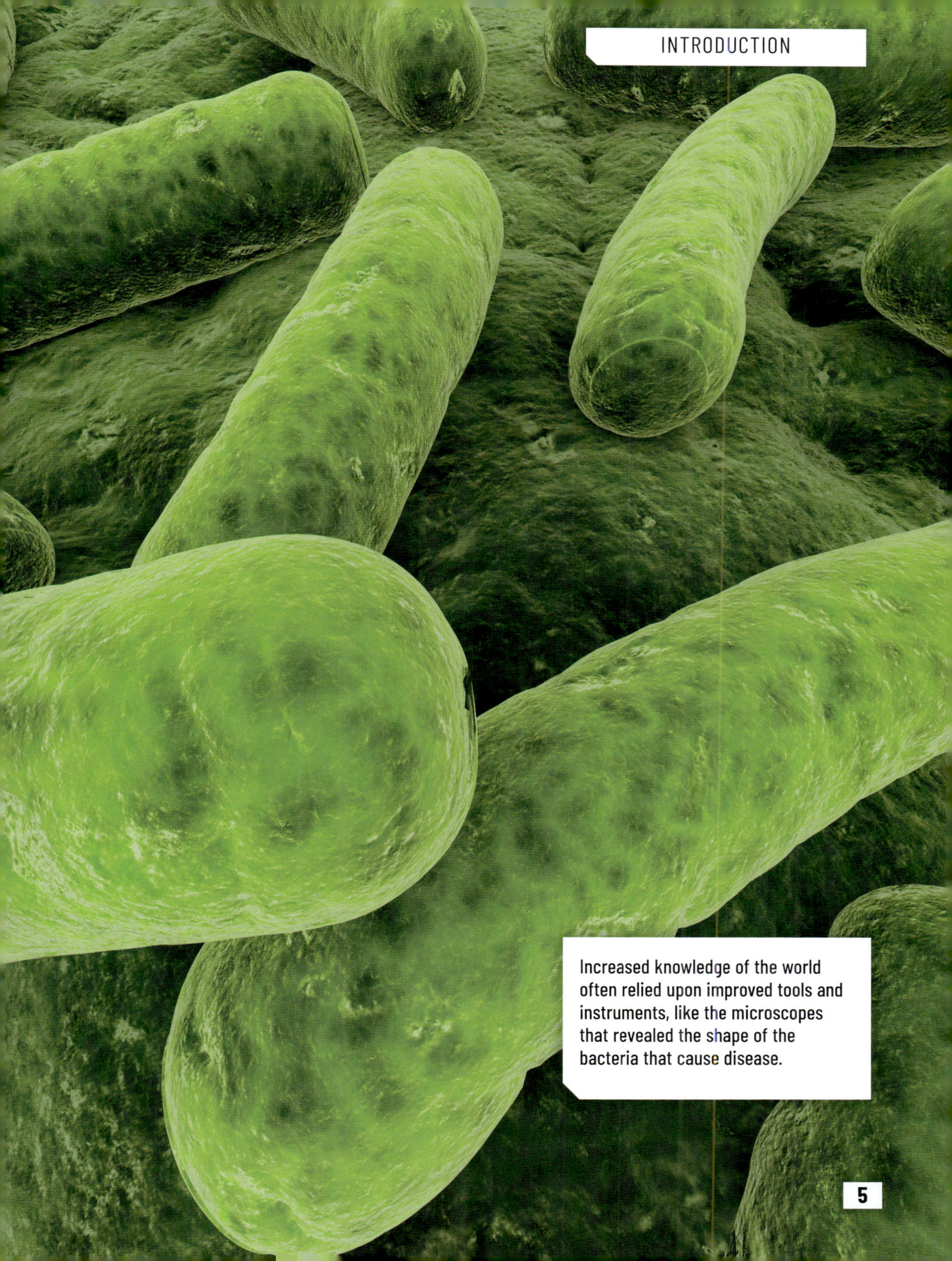

Increased knowledge of the world often relied upon improved tools and instruments, like the microscopes that revealed the shape of the bacteria that cause disease.

Evidence in Fossils

Fossils are the remains of plants and animals that have been dead for a very long time. They are usually the hard parts of animals that have been changed to rock.

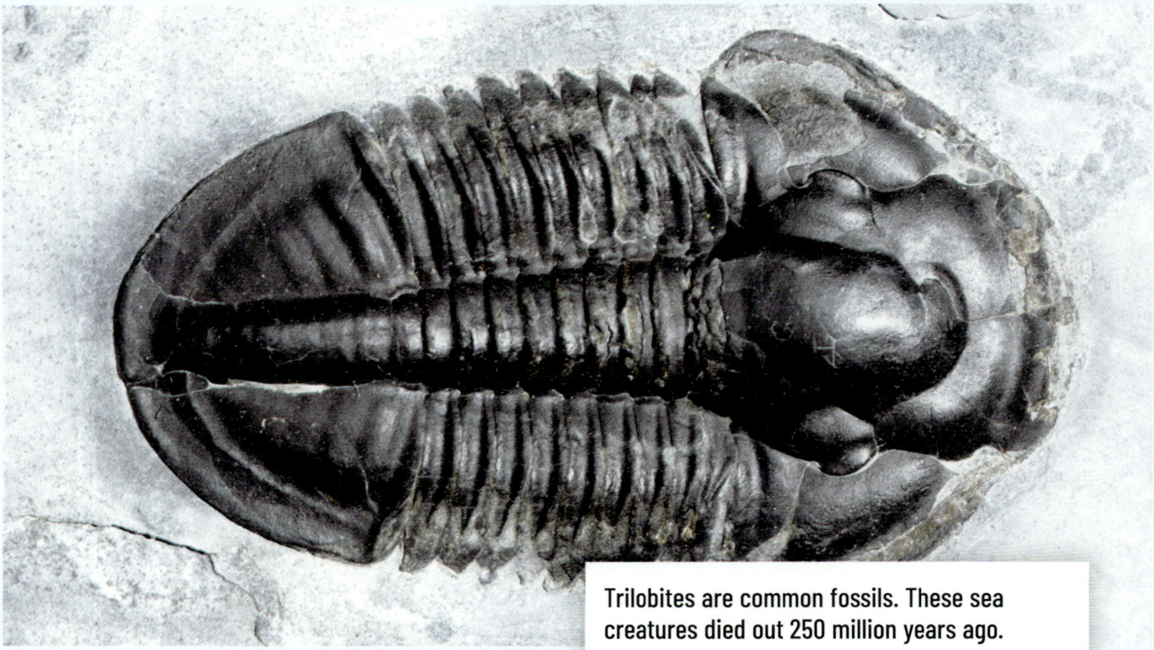

Trilobites are common fossils. These sea creatures died out 250 million years ago.

TIMELINE
1800–1803

KEY:

Biology and Medicine

Engineering and Invention

Astronomy and Math

Chemistry and Physics

1800 English astronomer William Herschel discovers infrared radiation (from the sun).

1800 Italian physicist Alessandro Volta invents the voltaic pile battery for producing a continuous electric current.

1800

1800 Italian astronomer Giuseppe Piazzi locates Ceres, the first asteroid (minor planet) to be discovered.

Ancient dinosaur bones preserved in stone.

In 1517, the Italian physician and poet Girolamo Fracastoro was probably the first person to suggest that fossils are the remains of living organisms. But no one took much notice at the time, and it was not until the fossil finds in Europe of the late 18th century that scientists began to realize that fossils can tell us a great deal about the history of living things and the rocks in which they are found.

In 1793, French naturalist Jean-Baptiste Lamarck (1744–1829) revived the idea that fossils represent ancient organisms, and this time other scientists began to listen to the argument. Two years later, another Frenchman, Georges Cuvier (1769–1832), discovered one of the first dinosaur fossils, although the word "dinosaur," which comes from Greek words meaning

Timeline

1517 Fracastoro suggests fossils are animal remains

1793 Lamarck revives Fracastoro's theory

1795 Cuvier discovers a dinosaur fossil

1811 Mary Anning discovers ichthyosaur fossil

1816 William Smith proposes fossil-rock date correlation

Mary Anning became one of the most successful 19th-century fossil hunters.

1801 English physicist Thomas Young observes the interference of light.

1802 French naturalist Jean-Baptiste Lamarck introduces the word "biology" for the study of living things and life processes.

1803 English chemist John Dalton proposes his atomic theory, that elements are indivisible atoms that combine to form compounds.

1803 German physician John Otto describes the inherited blood disorder hemophilia.

1803 English engineer Richard Trevithick makes the first steam-powered railroad locomotive.

1801 1802 1803

Mary Anning, Fossil Hunter

As sea cliffs become eroded by waves and weather, the sedimentary rocks release any fossils they contain. In 1811, schoolgirl Mary Anning was walking on a beach in Dorset, southern England, when she found a complete fossil skeleton of an ichthyosaur, a fishlike reptile that swam in the seas 150 million years ago during the Mesozoic Era. The enterprising 12-year-old sold her find to a museum and went on to become one of the world's best-known fossil collectors.

"terrible lizard," only came later when the English fossil hunter Richard Owen (1804–1892) invented the term in 1842.

How Fossils Form

Paleontologists (scientists who study fossils) discovered several ways in which fossils can form. The animal remains are buried quickly, before the carcass can decay or be eaten by scavengers. The best place for that to happen is underwater, in the mud or sediment at the bottom of a lake or sea. That is also the place where sedimentary rocks form. Remains embedded in sediment may be dissolved by water, leaving behind a perfect mold. Minerals may be deposited in the mold, forming a cast often made from a totally different type of rock than the sediment. Footprints or animal tracks in mud can be preserved in a similar way. Preserving a whole animal only happens occasionally when conditions are right, as when insects become trapped in amber (fossilized tree resin) or mammoths are buried in the permanently frozen ground of the permafrost. (Sometimes, human skeletons have been fossilized.) Tar pits in California have preserved some complete skeletons of prehistoric animals.

TIMELINE
1804–1807

KEY:
- Biology and Medicine
- Engineering and Invention
- Astronomy and Math
- Chemistry and Physics

1804 English inventor and founder of the science of aerodynamics George Cayley builds and flies a model glider.

1805 English naval officer Francis Beaufort devises the Beaufort scale for classifying the strength of winds.

1804

1805

1805 French inventor Joseph Jacquard constructs a loom that is controlled by a "chain" of punched cards.

1805 French naturalist Georges Cuvier founds the science of comparative anatomy.

This illustration shows a sequence of fossil formation.

Using Fossils for Dating

Over millions of years, sedimentary rocks form strata one above the other. As long as no great upheavals disturb them, younger rock layers always lie on top of older ones. In 1816, geologist William Smith showed that the age of a fossil must be the same as the rock in which it is found (and vice versa). This provided a new method of geological dating. The absolute dating of fossils and rocks had to await new 20th-century techniques such as dating by using radioactivity.

1. Coral skeletons (form reefs)
2. Silica skeleton of zooplankton
3. Ammonite shell
4. Bivalve (mollusk) shell
5. Trace fossils of tracks in mud
6. Graptolite (planktonlike) fossils
7. Petrified wood from tree
8. Carbonized leaves
9. Insect trapped in amber

1806 French chemists identify the first amino acid, asparagine (in asparagus).

1807 U.S. engineer Robert Fulton builds a successful paddle steamer, *Clermont*.

1806

1807

1806 Swiss mathematician Jean-Robert Argand devises the Argand diagram for representing complex numbers as points on a coordinate plane.

1807 The Royal Geological Society is founded in London, England.

William and Caroline Herschel

This brother-and-sister team pioneered powerful telescopes and identified Uranus, the first new planet to be discovered since ancient times.

William Herschel (1738–1822) and Caroline (1750–1848), his younger sister, were born in Hanover. At the time this was a German state ruled by the king of Great Britain. Herschel's father was a musician in the Hanover Military Band, and William also became a musician. When the French army invaded Hanover in 1757, William took refuge in England. William Herschel was fascinated by telescopes. He built one in 1774 and over the next nine years observed the nebulae (clouds of gas and dust) and double stars, two stars that

Music took second place to William Herschel's astronomical work.

TIMELINE
1808–1811

KEY:

- Biology and Medicine
- Engineering and Invention
- Astronomy and Math
- Chemistry and Physics

1808

1808 English chemist Humphry Davy invents the arc lamp.

1808 English inventor George Cayley builds an uncrewed glider.

1808 French physicist Siméon Poisson puts forward a theory to account for irregularities in the orbits of the planets.

appear close together when seen from Earth. Herschel achieved fame when he discovered a previously unknown object in the constellation of Gemini. This was soon confirmed as being a new planet, later called Uranus. The success that he now enjoyed enabled him

Timeline

1757 William Herschel arrives in England

1781 William discovers Uranus and becomes court astronomer

1786-97 Caroline Herschel discovers eight comets

1790 William finishes a 40-foot (12 m) reflecting telescope, the largest scientific instrument created to that point

1803 William publishes his account of 500 double star systems

An image of William Herschel's 40-foot (12 m) telescope, which was constructed in 1790.

1809 French naturalist Jean-Baptiste Lamarck proposes the (now discredited) theory that characteristics, such as a weightlifter's muscles, are passed on from parents to their offspring.

1810 French chef Nicolas Appert invents food canning (originally for Napoleon's army).

1810 German engineer Friedrich König invents a steam-powered printing press.

1811 Mary Anning discovers the first fossil of an ichthyosaur in southern England.

1811 Italian scientist Amedeo Avogadro proposes Avogadro's law: that at the same temperature and pressure, equal volumes of all gases contain the same number of molecules.

1811 William Herschel proposes a theory that stars develop from nebulae as clouds of gas condense into star clusters.

1809 1810 1811

The planet Uranus. Its discovery in 1781 made William Herschel famous.

to develop better telescopes through which he could observe the night sky in greater detail. His achievements included two extensive catalogues of nebulae in 1802 and 1820. He also realized that there was a previously unknown source of heat that we now know as infrared radiation, and described how the ice caps on Mars changed in size. He believed there was life on Mars, and perhaps even within the sun.

Caroline Herschel

William's sister Caroline arrived in England in 1772, after the death of her father. She looked after the house and helped her brother to construct new, more powerful telescopes. They created reflecting telescopes, in which the image from the sky is projected onto a mirror at the base of the telescope. The

TIMELINE
1813–1815

KEY:

- Biology and Medicine
- Engineering and Invention
- Astronomy and Math
- Chemistry and Physics

1813 Swiss botanist Augustin de Candolle devises a plant classification system, which he calls a "taxonomy."

1813 English engineer William Hedley builds his steam locomotive *Puffing Billy.*

1814 German physicist Joseph von Fraunhofer invents the spectroscope.

1814 Spanish-born physician Matthieu Orfila founds the modern science of toxicology, the study of poisons.

mirrors had to be extremely smooth, and the Herschels spent up to 16 hours per day grinding and polishing them. Caroline was successful in her own right. She found eight new comets, and King George III awarded her a salary to help her continue her work. After William's death, Caroline moved back to Hanover, where she continued to work on star catalogues. William's son, John, carried on their astronomical observations.

William and Caroline polishing the mirror for one of their telescopes. Their hard work paid off when they discovered many previously unidentified objects in the night sky.

1815 French physicist Augustin-Jean Fresnel discovers the diffraction of light as it passes through a small aperture.

1815 English scholar Peter Roget devises a slide rule with two logarithmic scales to help with multiplication and division.

1815

1815 In England, chemist Humphry Davy and engineer George Stephenson independently invent a safety lamp for miners.

1815 English geologist William Smith publishes a geological map of the rocks of England and Wales.

The Birth of Photography

The camera had its beginnings nearly 1,000 years before film, which had to wait for the discovery of light-sensitive chemicals that could "capture" the camera's image.

In 1843, William Fox Talbot set up a photographic "factory" in his greenhouse.

TIMELINE
1816–1819

KEY:
- Biology and Medicine
- Engineering and Invention
- Chemistry and Physics

1816 Scottish engineer Robert Stirling invents a two-cylinder external combustion engine.

1817 French chemists discover chlorophyll, the light-absorbing pigment in plants.

1817 French doctor René Laennec invents a stethoscope so he can amplify the heartbeats of a patient.

1818 Engineer Rudolph Ackermann devises a steering mechanism for horse-drawn carriages; it remains the basis of modern automobile steering.

Early cameras were big and clumsy to use; they had to be large enough to hold the photographic plates.

Timeline

1725 Light sensitivity of silver salts

1826 Niépce's first photograph

1839 Daguerreotypes

1841 Calotypes

1851 Wet-collodion process

1871 Dry gelatin plates

1888 First Kodak camera

The origin of the camera was the camera obscura (Latin for "dark room"), a windowless room with a small hole in one wall. Light entering the hole forms an upside-down image of the scene outside on the opposite wall. Artists used the device as an aid to trace an image, and later it became portable in the form of a large light-excluding box. In this version, a glass lens soon replaced the hole.

Fixing an Image on Paper

In 1725, the German physician Johann Schulze found that certain silver salts turn dark when exposed to daylight. Fifty years later, Swedish chemist Karl Scheele discovered that the darkening effect was due to the presence of grains of metallic silver. As a result, silver salts were to become standard ingredients in photographic emulsions (light-sensitive coatings) for films, paper, and even leather—as tried in the late 1790s by Englishman Thomas Wedgwood.

Artists used camera obscuras to draw outdoor scenes from indoors.

1819 British astronomer John Herschel discovers that sodium thiosulfate can "fix" a newly developed photographic image.

1819

1819 U.S. engineers Stephen McCormick and Jethro Wood independently produce a cast-iron plow.

1819 German inventor Augustus Siebe develops a pressurized diving suit complete with helmet.

How a Camera Obscura Works

In a portable camera obscura, a lens focuses light from a scene onto a mirror. The mirror, angled at 45 degrees, reflects the image upward onto a glass screen. An artist can then trace the image. This method may have been used by the painter Canaletto, who made detailed cityscapes. The camera obscura was used as an artist's aid until it was replaced by photographs after the 1850s.

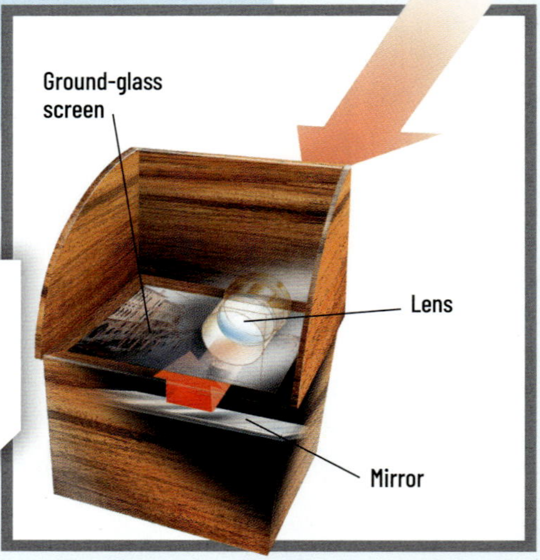

The portable camera obscura was a box fitted with a lens and a mirror.

In France, Joseph Niépce experimented with fleeting silver images. His first successful photograph in 1826 used a polished pewter plate coated with bitumen as the light-sensitive substance.

In 1839, Frenchman Louis Daguerre used iodine to make photographic plates. He exposed the plate in a camera and "developed" it in mercury vapor. The image was made permanent, or "fixed," in a solution of common salt. These daguerreotypes, as his images were known, were mirror images and could only be used once.

A Series of Improvements

In 1841, English chemist William Fox Talbot patented his calotype process. After exposure to light in a camera, the film was developed in a solution of gallic acid and fixed. The resulting "negative" image (with black and white reversed) was placed with a sheet of light-sensitive paper

TIMELINE
1820–1822

KEY:
- Biology and Medicine
- Engineering and Invention
- Astronomy and Math
- Chemistry and Physics

1820 The Royal Astronomical Society is founded in London.

1820 French chemists discover the alkaloid quinine, soon to be used to treat malaria.

1820

1820 Danish physicist Hans Ørsted discovers electromagnetism when he notices the needle of a compass is deflected by an electric current.

This daguerreotype of a street in Paris, made by Daguerre in 1839, is the first ever photograph to include a human being.

and changed back to positive. This stage could be repeated many times. Fox Talbot established himself as one of the world's first professional photographers, with a studio in Reading, southern England, where the rich and famous had their portraits taken between 1843 and 1847. The texture of the paper meant the prints remained slightly coarse. Frenchman Louis-Désiré Blanquart-Evrard made more improvements in 1850 by coating the printing paper with albumen (egg white).

A Londoner, Frederick Archer, invented the wet-collodion process in 1851. It was used until dry plates, using gelatin emulsions, had superseded it in the late 1870s. American George Eastman used a dry gelatin emulsion for his first Kodak camera of 1888, initially on paper film and a year later on transparent celluloid. With the Kodak, the era of mass-market photography had arrived.

1821 U.S. engineer Zachariah Allen installs the first hot-air central heating system.

1821 French astronomer Alexis Bouvard observes irregularities in the orbit of Uranus; they prove to be caused by the gravity of Neptune.

1821

1822 French naturalist Jean-Baptiste Lamarck distinguishes between vertebrates and invertebrates.

1822 English inventor Charles Babbage makes a mechanical adding machine, or "difference engine."

1822

Michael Faraday

Faraday was a physicist and a chemist, one of the greatest experimental scientists who ever lived. He founded the sciences of electromagnetism and electrochemistry.

Faraday's Christmas lectures presented science in a simple way to nonscientific audiences.

TIMELINE

1823–1826

KEY:

- Biology and Medicine
- Engineering and Invention
- Astronomy and Math
- Chemistry and Physics

1823 Scottish chemist Charles Macintosh invents and patents waterproof fabric made by coating cloth with rubber.

1823 The medical journal *The Lancet* is published for the first time in London.

1824 French physicist Dominique Arago discovers magnetic induction—the production of an electric field by a changing magnetic field.

1824 Swedish chemist Jöns Jacob Berzelius discovers silicon; a year later Danish physicist Hans Ørsted prepares an impure form of aluminum.

1823

1824

Michael Faraday, the son of a blacksmith, was born just outside London, England. At age 13, he left school to become an apprentice bookbinder. Reading some of the books stirred in him an interest in science. He even carried out simple experiments with electricity. In 1813, he became assistant to chemist Humphry Davy at the Royal Institution, where part of his job was to set up experiments for Davy's lectures. In 1827, he took over Davy's post of lecturer at the Royal Institution, becoming professor of chemistry there in 1833.

Timeline

1821 Simple electric motor

1823 Liquid chlorine

1825 Benzene

1831 Electromagnetic induction

1834 Laws of electrolysis

Chemical Discoveries

Faraday made several discoveries in chemistry. In 1823, he liquefied chlorine by heating it in a sealed tube; previously only two other gases had been liquefied. In 1825, Faraday discovered benzene. In 1834, he turned his attention to electrolysis, the process in which an electric current passing through a solution (electrolyte) between two electrodes brings about chemical change. Usually a gas is produced at either electrode, or a metal is deposited on the negatively charged cathode. The experiments led to Faraday's laws of electrolysis: 1. The amount of chemical change is proportional to the quantity of electricity; 2. The amount of change (produced by a fixed quantity of electricity) in

Michael Faraday's most important discovery was benzene, the first of the so-called aromatic hydrocarbons and the basis of a new branch of organic chemistry.

1825 French naturalist Georges Cuvier puts forward his catastrophe theory of extinction, that cataclysmic events cause species to become extinct.

1825 English chemist and physicist Michael Faraday discovers benzene and several of its compounds.

1826 French chemist Joseph Niépce takes the first photograph (on a metal plate).

1826 German astronomer Heinrich Olbers puts forward his famous paradox: Why is the sky dark at night when the universe is full of stars?

1825 1826

different substances is proportional to the equivalent weight of the substance.

The Electric Motor

In physics, Faraday made the first primitive electric motor in 1821. He suspended a length of stiff wire next to a bar magnet that projected vertically from a dish of mercury. When he connected a battery between the mercury and the top of the wire, the lower end of the wire rotated around the magnet. In 1831, Faraday wound two separate coils of wire around an iron ring. He connected one

Magnetic Fields

Surrounding every magnet is a field of force known as a magnetic field. Faraday studied the interaction between such fields and electric currents flowing in wires and other conductors. This branch of physics is now called electromagnetism. It is the basis of most electrical machines, from motors and dynamos to the electric bell, the relay, and the solenoid (a type of electric switch).

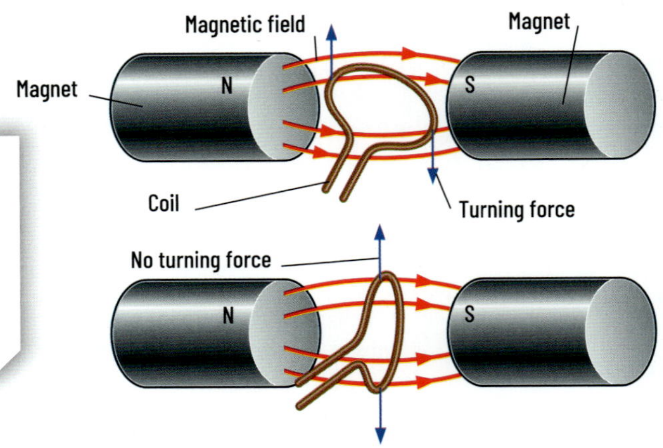

The angle of the coil dictates whether or not a magnetic field produces a turning force (top) or not (below).

TIMELINE
1827–1830

KEY:

- Biology and Medicine
- Engineering and Invention
- Astronomy and Math
- Chemistry and Physics

1827 U.S. artist John James Audubon publishes the first part of *Birds of America*.

1828 Estonian naturalist Karl von Baer founds the science of embryology.

1828 French physiologist Pierre Flourens explains how the semicircular canals in the inner ear control the sense of balance.

The candle was the subject of one of Faraday's most popular lectures.

wire to a galvanometer (an instrument that detects an electric current). When he connected a battery to the other wire, the galvanometer needle registered a current. He also showed that when a magnet is moved in and out of a wire coil, a current is generated in the coil. Faraday had discovered electromagnetic induction.

Faraday made many lasting contributions, including the children's Christmas lectures, which he started at the Royal Institution in 1826 and which he continued for 19 years. His "The Chemical History of a Candle" is still published, and eminent scientists still give the lectures. Faraday's name is commemorated in two scientific units. The farad is the SI unit of capitance; the Faraday constant is the electric charge carried by 1 mole of electrons or singly charged ions.

The Principle of the Electric Motor

Faraday demonstrated the principle of the electric motor with this simple apparatus. A copper rod, pivoted at the top, dips into a pool of mercury alongside a vertical magnet. When a current flows along the rod, the rod rotates around the magnet.

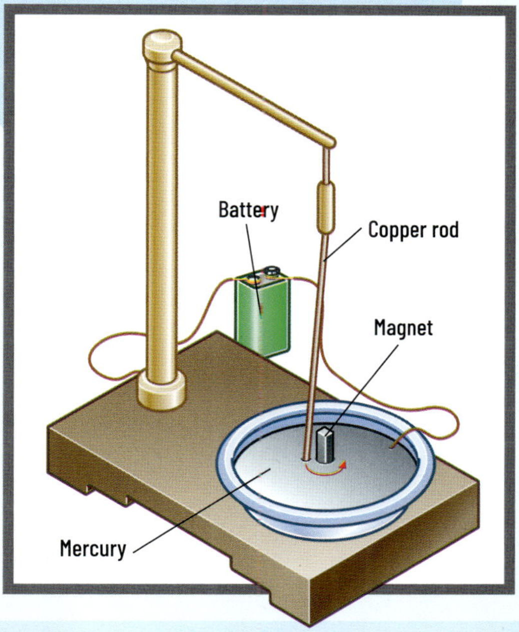

1829 Blind French teacher Louis Braille invents the Braille alphabet to allow blind people to read.

1830 U.S. engineer Peter Cooper builds *Tom Thumb*, the first locomotive to be made in North America.

1830 Scottish chemist Andrew Ure invents the bimetallic strip thermostat.

1829

1830

1829 George Stephenson's *Rocket* locomotive wins trials to provide the power for the Liverpool & Manchester Railway.

1830 Scottish writer Mary Somerville publishes a book of popular astronomy, *The Mechanism of the Heavens*.

Jöns Jacob Berzelius

Berzelius was a Swedish chemist who discovered new elements and promoted international cooperation in scientific research.

Jöns Jacob Berzelius (1779–1848) was a key figure in the great advancements made in chemistry during the 1800s. He was the son of a teacher, studied medicine, and became a physician in 1802. He also became interested in many aspects of contemporary scientific research, including electricity. When he found out about Volta's electric pile, for example, he made a battery for himself. He even performed experiments using electricity to treat some of his medical patients.

Jöns Jacob Berzelius was a major force in chemistry during the first half of the 19th century.

TIMELINE
1831–1834

KEY:

Engineering and Invention

Astronomy and Math

Chemistry and Physics

1831 English naval officer James Ross locates the position of the magnetic north pole (which constantly changes).

1831

1831 English scientist Michael Faraday makes a simple dynamo.

1832

1832 French chemist Pierre Robiquet discovers codeine (in opium from poppies).

A sample of silicon. Berzelius discovered this important element in 1824.

International Cooperation

Berzelius's interest in science led to his being appointed secretary of the Royal Swedish Academy of Sciences in 1818, a post he held until his death. He was determined to work with other international scientists, believing that new theories could only be accepted if they were

Timeline

1802 Berzelius qualifies as a medical doctor

1808 Joins the Royal Swedish Academy of Sciences

1812 Visits Britain where he meets Humphry Davy, William Herschel, and James Watt

1818 Becomes secretary of the Royal Swedish Academy of Sciences

1822 Begins an annual series of reports that present chemical research in Europe during the previous year

1836 Describes the use of catalysts, substances that speed up chemical reactions, but which are not themselves changed

1833 English mathematician Charles Babbage begins work on his "analytical engine," a type of mechanical computer (which he never finishes).

1833 U.S. engineer Obed Hussey invents a reaping machine.

1834 U.S. engineer Cyrus McCormick patents a reaping and binding machine, an early form of combine harvester.

1834 English scientist Michael Faraday formulates the laws of electrolysis.

1833

1834

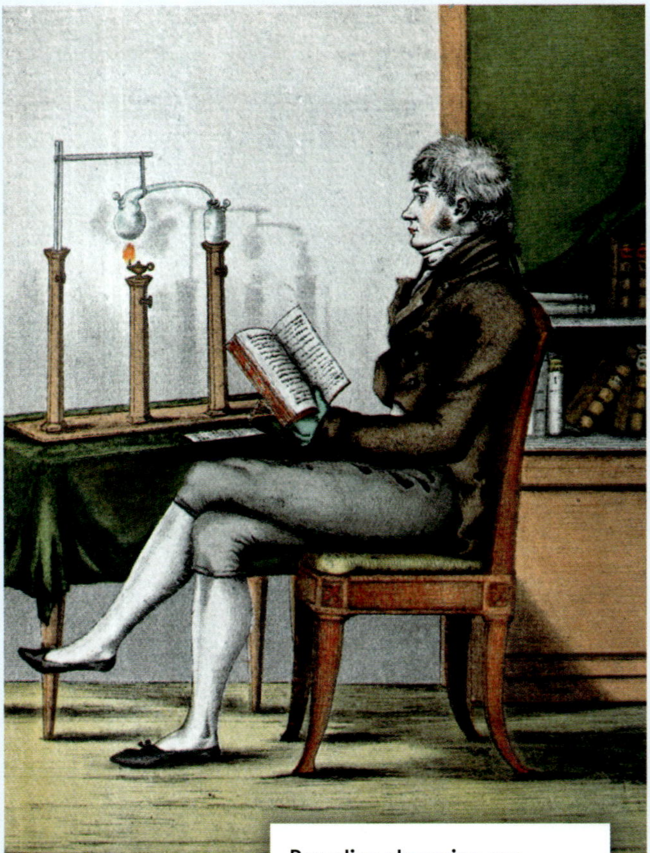

Berzelius observing one of his many experiments.

tested in many places. He spent time in laboratories in England, Germany, and France, and wrote many letters to well-respected scientists of the day. Berzelius is best known for his invention of the modern way of writing symbols for chemical elements, using simple one- or two-letter descriptions, along with the number of atoms of that substance in a compound. So, H_2O shows that there are two hydrogen atoms for each oxygen atom in water.

Atomic Weight

Perhaps Berzelius's most important contribution to science was his creation of a list of the atomic weights of all the then known elements, using oxygen as weighing 100. This list helped to show that inorganic chemical compounds are made up of elements combining in whole numbers of atoms. This work also led him to make a vital distinction

TIMELINE
1835–1838

KEY:

Biology and Medicine

Engineering and Invention

Chemistry and Physics

1835 U.S. manufacturer Samuel Colt produces a revolver with interchangeable parts.

1835

1835 English photographer William Fox Talbot invents the calotype process, which produces paper negatives from which multiple photographic prints can be made.

between organic compounds (those containing carbon) and inorganic compounds (those not including carbon).

Berzelius himself discovered some new elements, including cerium and selenium, while students working with him discovered lithium, lanthanum, and vanadium. He diligently kept track of the hundreds of experiments performed by his students and collaborators. He observed and noted how these experiments either agreed with or contradicted each other.

Humphry Davy, a British chemist Berzelius admired. Davy and Berzelius disagreed over whether chlorine should be classed as an element. Davy claimed it was an element in 1810, but Berzelius believed it contained oxygen and so was a compound. In 1816, however, Berzelius admitted he had been wrong after experiments showed chlorine did not contain oxygen.

1836 U.S. engineer Thomas Davenport makes a model streetcar.

1836 English naturalist Charles Darwin completes his voyage on HMS *Beagle*.

1836 Swedish chemist Jöns Berzelius discovers catalysts, which speed up chemical reactions.

1837 U.S. industrialist John Deere invents a steel plow.

1838 French chemist Anselme Payen identifies cellulose, the basic material of all plants.

1838 U.S. inventor Samuel Morse demonstrates his electric telegraph and the Morse code that it uses.

1836 1837 1838

Darwin and Evolution

In 1831, Charles Darwin set sail on HMS *Beagle*. The observations he made during the voyage eventually led to his theory of evolution through natural selection.

Darwin plays with a monkey companion in this cartoon. Darwin's idea that humans shared a common ancestor with apes was widely mocked in popular magazines of the day.

TIMELINE
1839–1841

KEY:
- Biology and Medicine
- Engineering and Invention
- Chemistry and Physics

1839 U.S. inventor Charles Goodyear develops a process to harden rubber.

1839 German biologist Theodor Schwann suggests that all living matter is made up of cells.

1839

1839 French chemist Louis Daguerre invents the daguerreotype, a type of photograph taken on metal plates.

Charles Darwin (1809–1882), grandson of English physician Erasmus Darwin, was 22 years old when he joined HMS *Beagle*. The young man's duty was to provide company for the ship's captain, because the conventions of the time did not allow the captain to socialize with his officers or crew.

Darwin wanted to be a naturalist, and he used the five-year voyage to study plants and animals in faraway places. The ship visited islands off the west coast of Africa before sailing around Cape Horn and up the western coast of South America. It then stopped in the Galápagos Islands before sailing across the Pacific to Tahiti and New Zealand. It headed back to England by way of Mauritius and South Africa. At each stop, Darwin went ashore to observe local flora and fauna and collect specimens of rocks, plants, and animals.

Timeline

1831–1836 Voyage of HMS *Beagle*

1838 Reads *An Essay on the Principle of Population* by Thomas Malthus

1858 Joint paper with naturalist Alfred Russel Wallace

1859 Publishes *On the Origin of Species*

Observing Animals

In South America, Darwin spent more time on land than on the ship. He studied the rocks and geology of the places he visited as well. In Patagonia, he found a shore with a 19.6-foot-high (6 m) cliff that contained some huge bones. They were

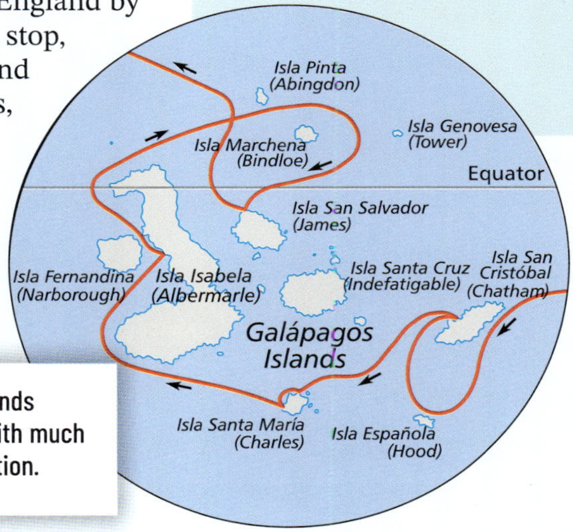

The Galápagos Islands provided Darwin with much evidence for evolution.

1840 German pathologist Jacob Henle puts forward his germ theory of disease: that infection is caused by parasitic organisms invading the body.

1841 English engineer Joseph Whitworth introduces a system of standard screw threads.

1840

1841

1840 German chemist Christian Schönbein discovers and names ozone.

The Finches of the Galápagos Islands

In the Galápagos, Darwin found species of finches that differed only in coloration and the shapes of their beaks. The finches that ate seeds had short, stubby beaks, while birds that ate insects had long, thin beaks. Darwin deduced that they were variations of a species that had gradually evolved beaks appropriate to their chosen food.

Finches 1, 3, and 4 have long beaks for eating insects; finch 2 is a fruit-eating species; and the beaks of finches 5 and 6 are best at tackling seeds.

too large to belong to any living creature. Darwin observed that, apart from size, they resembled the bones of South American armadillos and sloths. He realized that their giant ancestors had become extinct, but why?

The *Beagle* returned to England in the fall of 1836, and Darwin moved to London. He studied geology and was converted to the ideas of geologist Charles Lyell, who argued the world was in a constant state of change.

Forming a Theory

Darwin's main concern was animal species; what happens when species produce many offspring when there is insufficient food for all of them? Darwin's idea was that only the fittest animals survive, and that they did so because a process he called natural selection was taking place. "Nature"—that is, an individual's strength or adaptability—decided which animals survived. At the

TIMELINE

1842–1844

KEY:

- Biology and Medicine
- Engineering and Invention
- Chemistry and Physics

1842 German physicist Julius von Mayer states the principle of the conservation of energy (that energy can be neither created nor destroyed, merely changed from one form to another).

1842 U.S. surgeon Crawford Long uses ether as an anesthetic.

1842

1842 Black American inventor Norbert Rillieux designs a vacuum evaporator for extracting juice from sugarcane.

1842 Charles Bell identifies and describes Bell's palsy, which can paralyze the face.

same time Darwin was at work, Welsh naturalist Alfred Russel Wallace came to similar conclusions based on his observations of Asian and Australasian animals. He wrote about his theories in 1858 and sent them to Darwin. The pair met and issued a joint paper.

In 1859, Darwin published his epic *On the Origin of Species by Means of Natural Selection*. He argued that evolution takes place in stages by chance mutations. Favorable mutations are inherited and passed on to offspring to produce a gradual change in a whole species. Eventually new, fitter species come into existence and old, less fit ones become extinct. Darwin and his contemporaries had no idea exactly how such mutations take place. Unknown to them, heredity was being studied in an Austrian monastery by the monk Gregor Mendel. He grew generations of pea plants to figure out the basic laws of heredity—how offspring receive sets of inherited "factors" that we now call genes. Genetics is the means by which evolution takes place.

Darwin's Ideas and Human Society

Some thinkers tried to apply Darwin's theory of "the survival of the fittest" to human society. This theory, or Social Darwinism, argued that it was right that some people—the "fittest"—became successful while others remained poor. The theory was popular for a time, as it seemed to explain the wide differences between individuals' success and wealth. It was later rejected in favor of a more inclusive view, in which the rich help support the poor.

The Galápagos were so remote that species had evolved there in isolation.

1843 The world's first underwater tunnel is built beneath the Thames River in London.

1844 U.S. inventor Samuel Morse sends the first message by telegraph in the United States.

1843

1844

1844 U.S. dentist Horace Wells uses nitrous oxide ("laughing gas") as an anesthetic.

Mendel and Genetics

Today, genetics is one of the major scientific disciplines. But it had humble beginnings in an Austrian monastery garden where Gregor Mendel grew pea plants.

Genetics would eventually explain why family members look like one another.

TIMELINE

1845–1847

KEY:

- Biology and Medicine
- Engineering and Invention
- Astronomy and Math
- Chemistry and Physics

1845 German zoologist Karl Siebold shows that protozoa are single-celled organisms.

1845 German physicist Franz Neumann publishes his theory of electromagnetic induction.

1845

1845 British engineer Isambard Brunel launches the first successful propeller-driven ship, SS *Great Britain*.

1845 French physicists take detailed photographs of the sun.

Gregor Mendel (1822–1884) was born in Austrian Silesia (now the Czech Republic). He studied at college before becoming an Augustinian monk in 1843. He became interested in hybrids—plants grown by crossing two different species—and began to breed pea plants in 1856. Over the next six years he grew 30,000 plants, which he fertilized artificially by transferring pollen from one plant to another. He crossed tall plants with short plants. He then counted the number of tall and short plants in the next and later generations. He found that all first-generation plants were tall, but the second generation had tall plants and short plants in the ratio of 3 to 1.

Timeline

1856 Mendel begins experiments with pea plants

1865 Reports to Brünn Natural History Society

1866 Publishes his results

1900 De Vries, Correns, and Tschermak-Seysenegg confirm Mendel's findings

Factors of Inheritance

Mendel concluded that every plant receives two "factors" of inheritance, one from each parent. In the first generation of peas in the example, each plant receives one factor for tallness from the tall parent and one factor for shortness from the short parent. But all the offspring are tall since the tallness factor is dominant over the shortness factor (which is known as recessive). Recessive factors can become dominant when two occur in a single individual, as in short plants of the second generation.

Gregor Mendel's experiments with pea plants laid the foundations for the modern science of genetics.

1846 U.S. inventor Elias Howe invents a lock-stitch sewing machine.

1846 German astronomer Johann Galle is the first person to observe the planet Neptune.

1846 The Smithsonian Institution is founded in Washington, D.C.

1847 The American Medical Association is founded in Philadelphia.

The Calico Cat

Genes for black and ginger pigments are carried on the X chromosome. Black (B) is dominant over ginger (b). Females have two X chromosomes, so they can be black (BB), ginger (bb), or calico (Bb). Males have only one X (and one Y), so they can only be black (B) or ginger (b). Males cannot be calico—which needs one black (B) and one ginger (b) allele—because they have only one X chromosome.

This diagram shows how calico cats get their mixture of black and ginger colors.

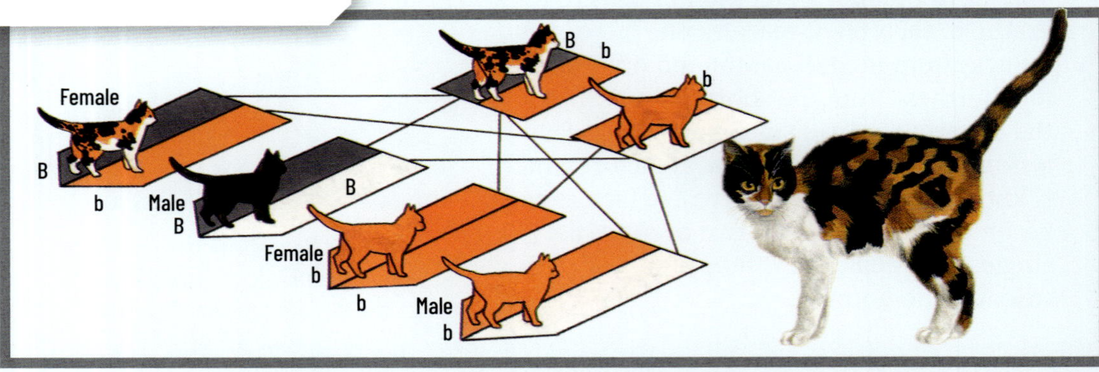

Mendel proposed two laws. The law of segregation states that the two factors controlling each hereditary characteristic segregate and pass into separate germ cells (egg and sperm). The law of independent assortment states that the pairs of factors segregate independently of each other during the formation of germ cells. He reported his results in 1865, publishing them a year later.

Building on Mendel's Work

Mendel's "factors" are now called alleles, which are alternative forms of a gene. There are two alleles of each gene in any cell, one inherited from each parent, which occupy the same place on a chromosome. Usually one

TIMELINE
1848–1850

KEY:
- Biology and Medicine
- Engineering and Invention
- Chemistry and Physics

1848 U.S. inventor James Bogardus introduces a method of making cast-iron buildings.

1848 Scottish physicist William Thomson, Lord Kelvin, introduces the absolute temperature (or Kelvin) scale.

1849 Swiss embryologist Rudolf von Kölliker states that nerve endings are extensions of nerve cells.

1849 Anglo-American engineer James Francis makes an improved reaction water turbine.

allele is dominant, and the other is recessive. A germ cell (gamete)—egg or sperm—has one allele. When egg and sperm combine at fertilization, the two alleles come together in a new individual that inherits characteristics from each parent. The appearance of the new individual depends on which characteristic (if any) is dominant.

After Mendel's death, several biologists studied inheritance. In Holland, Hugo de Vries came up with identical results to Mendel's. Then, German botanist Karl Correns and Austrian botanist Erich von Tschermak-Seysenegg published observations that confirmed Mendel had been right.

Predicting Colors of Pea Plants

The diagram below shows how Mendel's laws allow us to predict the colors that will be produced by crossing purple-flowered pea plants with white-flowered pea plants. Purple is dominant, and the first generation (known as F1 phenotypes) produced by planting seeds from the cross are all purple. But when this first generation is interbred in turn, the second generation (known as F2 phenotypes) has purple or white flowers in the ratio 3 purple to 1 white.

Pea plants grow quickly, so Mendel was easily able to check his theory and predictions.

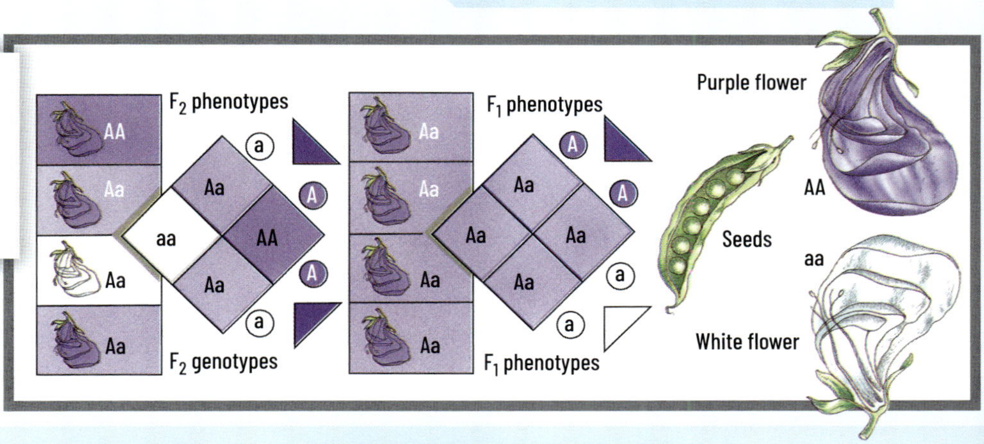

1850 English physician Alfred Higginson invents the hypodermic needle, initially for extracting samples of blood.

c.1850 German chemist Robert Bunsen begins using the Bunsen burner.

1850

1850 German physicist Rudolf Clausius formulates the second law of thermodynamics. It states that heat will not on its own move from a hot object to a hotter one.

The Periodic Table

By 1869, following many new discoveries, there were 63 known chemical elements. From these, Dmitri Mendeleyev constructed his famous periodic table.

Mendeleyev's periodic table later provided an insight into atomic structure.

TIMELINE
1851–1854

KEY:
- Biology and Medicine
- Engineering and Invention
- Astronomy and Math
- Chemistry and Physics

1851 French physicist Léon Foucault constructs Foucault's pendulum and uses it to prove the rotation of Earth.

1851 U.S. inventor Isaac Singer makes a single-thread sewing machine.

1852 U.S. inventor Elisha Otis patents the safety elevator.

1851

1852

Russian chemist Dmitri Mendeleyev (1834–1907) was born in Tobolsk, Siberia, the youngest child of a large middle-class family. Despite the death of his father when Dmitri was 13, his mother was determined that her youngest son should receive good schooling. He won a place at the Pedagogical Institute in St. Petersburg, a center for teacher training, qualifying as a teacher in 1855. He later studied chemistry at the University of St. Petersburg and in Germany. He took up a university post at St. Petersburg, and in 1869 began writing a textbook on chemistry (what we would call today inorganic chemistry).

Timeline

1869 Mendeleyev's periodic table

1875 Lecoq de Boisbaudran discovers gallium

1879 Nilson discovers scandium

1886 Winkler discovers germanium

1955 Discovery of mendelevium

Making the Table

Wishing to find order in the jumble of elements, he wrote the name of each one on a card. He then dealt sets of "hands," like dealing out playing cards. He arranged the elements in order of increasing atomic weight (the average mass of an atom of the element). He saw that if he started a new

Mendeleyev's work laid the foundations for all modern chemistry.

1853 English inventor George Cayley constructs a glider strong enough to carry a person.

1854 English mathematician George Boole introduces Boolean algebra, later important in the development of computer circuits.

1853

1854

1854 British physician John Snow finds a link between cholera and contaminated drinking water in London.

1854 U.S. chemist David Alter studies atomic spectra, the light given off by super-heated elements, and uses them as a method of chemical analysis.

The Modern Periodic Table

Today's periodic table contains many more elements than in Mendeleyev's time. They are arranged in order of their atomic numbers in seven horizontal "periods" of varying length. Two long series of 14 elements each—the lanthanides and the actinides—are shown in separate lines on page 37. The system of using a letter or letters to denote the symbol for each element (for example, Fe = iron) was introduced by the Swedish chemist Jöns Jacob Berzelius (1779–1848) in 1818.

row of cards every eighth element, those with similar chemical properties fell one above the other in columns.

Mendeleyev saw that properties tended to recur along each row—there was a "periodicity" in the properties. He named his new grid of rows and columns the periodic table. He even included in the table additional "missing" elements that were still to be discovered. He predicted the chemical and physical properties of these elements, their atomic weights, and melting points. In 1875, French chemist Paul Lecoq de Boisbaudran discovered "eka-aluminum" (in a space below aluminum), naming it gallium; in 1879, Swedish chemist Lars Nilson discovered "eka-boron"(below boron), and named it scandium; and in 1886, German chemist Clemens Winkler discovered "eka-silicon" (below silicon) and named it germanium. Mendeleyev's predictions had been fulfilled. By 1914, there were only seven gaps left in the table remaining up to element 92.

Atomic Structure

The atomic number is the total number of protons in an atom of any element. The modern periodic table is better described as being arranged in order of atomic number. In recent times, chemists have introduced the term "neutron number" (number of neutrons in the atom's nucleus)

TIMELINE
1855–1856

KEY:
Biology and Medicine
Engineering and Invention
Chemistry and Physics

1855 A design for a safety match is patented by Swedish chemist Johan Lundström.

1855 German pathologist Rudolph Virchow observes that cells originate from the division of other cells.

1855

1855 Italian physicist Luigi Palmieri designs a seismograph for measuring earthquakes.

1855 English physicist John Pratt shows that gravity remains constant everywhere at sea level.

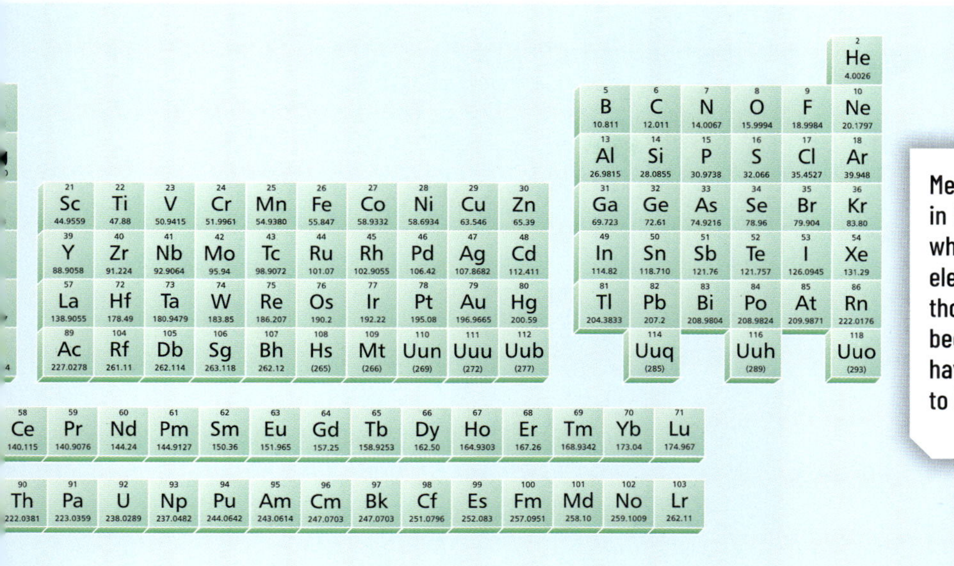

Mendeleyev left gaps in his periodic table where he thought new elements would fit: all those gaps have now been filled. New elements have also been added to Mendeleyev's table.

and call atomic weights "relative atomic masses." Mendeleyev could not explain the reason for the periodicity of the elements. That had to await an understanding of the structure of atoms, particularly how electrons arrange themselves around the nucleus of an atom. In the 20th century, chemists realized that the periodic table reflected the atomic structures of the elements as electrons fill up shells surrounding the nucleus. The periodic table enables chemists to predict more accurately what reactions are possible. In 1955, Mendeleyev received the ultimate honor when the element 101 was named mendelevium.

1856 Neanderthal remains are discovered in Germany.

1856 English steelmaker Henry Bessemer develops the Bessemer converter for making steel out of iron.

1856

1856 English chemist William Perkin invents mauveine, the first synthetic dye, which becomes the basis of a huge industry.

Germs and Disease

During the middle of the 19th century, scientists finally realized that germs cause most diseases and no longer blamed "evil spirits" or "bad air."

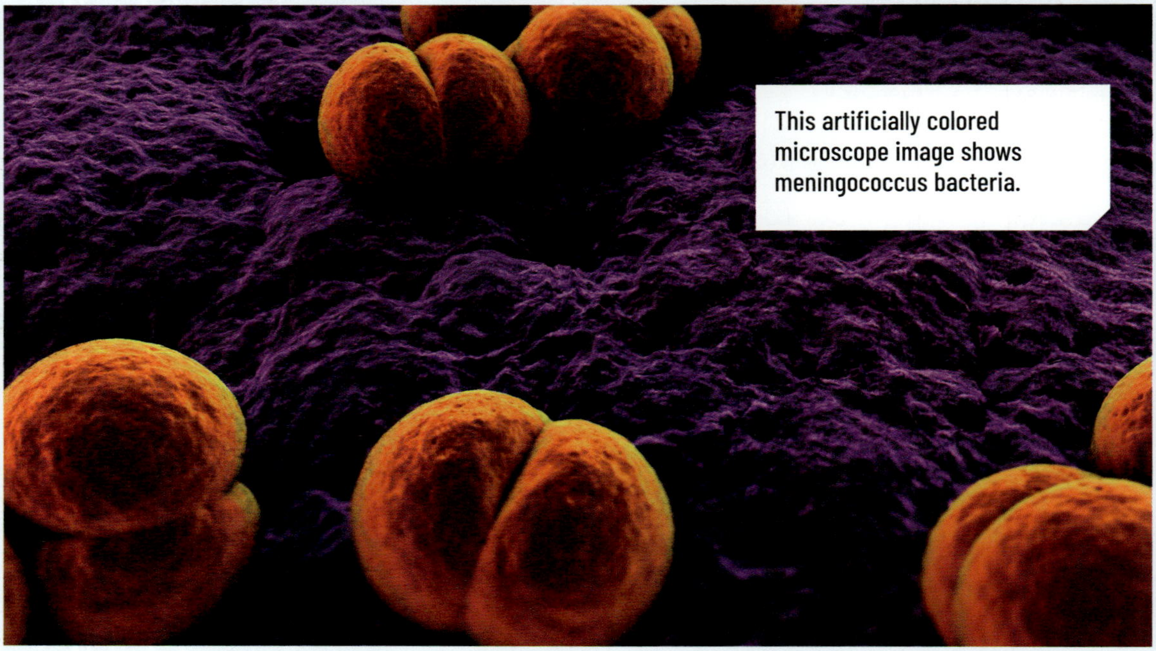

This artificially colored microscope image shows meningococcus bacteria.

TIMELINE
1857–1860

KEY:
- Biology and Medicine
- Engineering and Invention
- Chemistry and Physics

1857 French chemist Louis Pasteur observes that microorganisms cause fermentation.

1858 English anatomist Henry Gray publishes his famous book, *Anatomy of the Human Body*, or *Gray's Anatomy*.

1858 The first transatlantic submarine telegraph cable is laid.

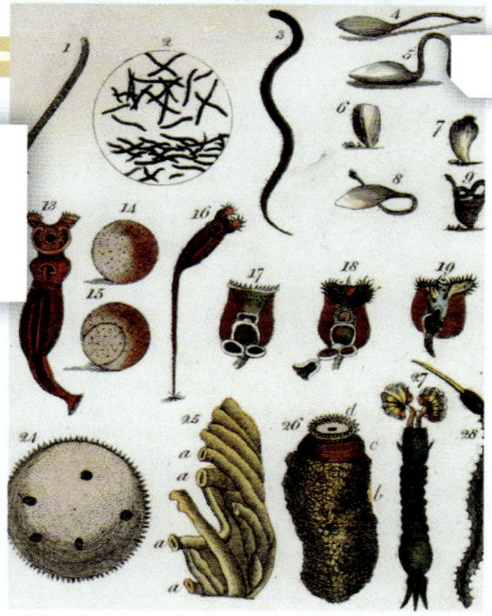

A 19th-century drawing shows "animacules" of varying shapes and sizes.

As early as 1546, Italian physician Girolamo Fracastoro had suggested in *On Contagion and Contagious Diseases* that germs are the cause of disease. Nobody took much notice, even after 1676, when Dutch scientist Antonie van Leeuwenhoek first saw bacteria, using the microscope he had made. The bacteria were from his own mouth and were probably not disease-carrying.

Timeline

1546 Fracastoro suggests germs cause disease

1676 Van Leeuwenhoek discovers bacteria

1840 Henle's germ theory of disease

1884 Gram's stain to classify bacteria

1897 Beijerinck discovers viruses

Germ Theory of Disease

In 1840, German pathologist Jacob Henle put forward the idea that infection is caused by parasitic organisms, the so-called germ theory of disease, which was later proposed independently by French chemist Louis Pasteur. In 1877, German bacteriologist Robert Koch announced that bacteria could be stained to make them easier to study under a microscope. Seven years later, Danish physician

Antonie van Leeuwenhoek made this microscope. He was the first person to observe bacteria.

1859 Charles Darwin publishes *On the Origin of Species*, the book in which he puts forward his theory of evolution.

1859 The world's first productive oil well is drilled in Pennsylvania by Edwin Drake.

1860 German scientists Robert Bunsen and Gustav Kirchhoff develop a method of analyzing substances by their spectra.

1860 English nurse Florence Nightingale sets up the first training school for nurses, in London, England.

Viruses

Viruses evaded discovery until the late 19th century. They turned out to have various shapes and to consist of an outer "container" of protein holding a molecule of DNA (deoxyribonucleic acid) or RNA (ribonucleic acid). They cannot multiply outside a living cell; but once they force their way into a cell, they make it produce more virus particles that break out and then invade other cells.

Louis Pasteur used rabbits and other animals in his studies of bacteria.

Hans Gram extended this idea as a means of classifying bacteria, which since then have been dubbed either Gram-positive or Gram-negative depending on their capacity to absorb a special stain. Bacteriologists also classify bacteria according to shape: coccus (round), bacillus (oval), spirochete (spiral), and so on.

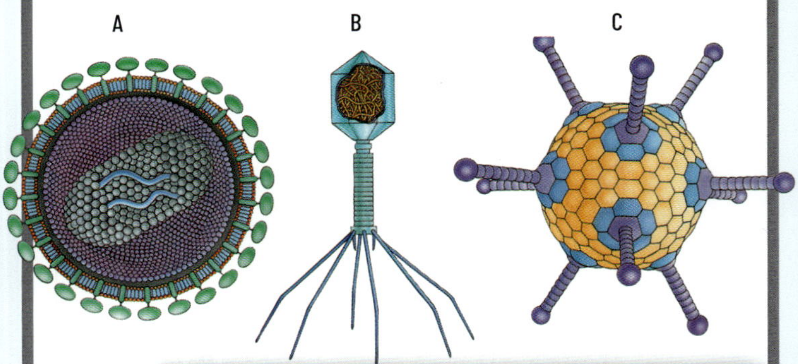

Shown here are an adenovirus (A), a bacteriophage (B), and HIV (human immunodeficiency virus).

Once biologists knew what bacteria looked like, the hunt was on. Scientists who handled cultures of infectious diseases often put themselves at great risk, but results came quickly. In 1880, German bacteriologist Karl Eberth found the bacillus that causes typhoid. In 1882, fellow German scientist Robert Koch

TIMELINE

1861–1863

KEY:

- Biology and Medicine
- Engineering and Invention
- Astronomy and Math
- Chemistry and Physics

1861 In Australia, the first large-scale food-freezing plant is built to prepare meat for export to Britain.

1861

1861 English physicist William Crookes uses spectrography to identify the element thallium.

found the bacterium that causes tuberculosis, while German researchers also identified the cause of the animal disease glanders. In 1897, Danish veterinarian Bernhard Bang discovered a bacillus that causes abortion in cattle, and the Japanese bacteriologist Kiyoshi Shiga found the cause of endemic dysentery.

Robert Koch discovered the bacterium that causes tuberculosis. His breakthrough was the first step in finding a cure for one of the biggest killers of the 19th century.

Other Microorganisms

Bacteria are not the only parasitic microorganisms to cause human diseases. Protozoans, for example, include the trypanosomes that cause sleeping sickness and Chagas disease, the amoebas that result in amebic dysentery, and the Plasmodium parasite responsible for malaria. Some microscopic fungi produce diseases that affect the skin or lungs. Most of these microorganisms were tracked down by 19th-century microbiologists.

In 1897, Dutch microbiologist Martinus Beijerinck proved that the microorganism causing tobacco mosaic disease escapes through a filter that traps bacteria. He had discovered the first virus. Since then, viruses have been found to be responsible for many diseases in humans, including yellow fever, influenza, polio, measles, and AIDS (acquired immune deficiency syndrome). Almost as fast as bacteriologists found bacteria, they developed vaccines against them. Vaccines for virus diseases proved more difficult, but now exist for many disorders.

1862 Swedish astronomer Anders Angström uses a spectroscope to identify hydrogen in the sun's atmosphere.

1862 U.S. gunsmith Richard Gatling patents a 10-barrel machine gun.

1863 Swedish chemist Alfred Nobel begins experimenting with the explosive nitroglycerin.

1863 French chemist Louis Pasteur introduces pasteurization, a process that kills bacteria in food and drink.

1863 The world's first underground railroad, the Metropolitan Line, opens in London.

1862

1863

Lister and Antiseptics

Joseph Lister used the germ theory of disease to make surgery and hospital treatment many times safer for patients than it had been before.

Until the mid-1800s, hospitals were dangerous places in Europe. Diseases spread rapidly and wounds were likely to become infected, particularly after surgery, often leading to death. Although scientists such as Antonie van Leeuwenhoek had identified bacteria as early as 1667, no one knew bacteria caused infection and disease. One reason for this was medical theory from the ideas of Galen in about 180 CE, which claimed that pus in wounds actually aided healing.

Joseph Lister realized that germs in the air, or carried on the hands and clothes of physicians, caused many of the infections that killed patients after surgery.

TIMELINE
1864–1867

KEY:

- Biology and Medicine
- Engineering and Invention
- Astronomy and Math
- Chemistry and Physics

1864 Scottish physicist James Clerk Maxwell publishes Maxwell's equations, which describe mathematically electromagnetic phenomena.

1864 French engineer Pierre Michaux makes the first pedal bicycle.

1865 Austrian monk Gregor Mendel formulates his laws of inheritance.

1865 U.S. locksmith Linus Yale perfects the cylinder lock and receives a second patent for it.

Ignaz Semmelweiss realized in the 1840s that washing hands was a simple way to lessen the risk of infections in women who had just given birth. However, he was mocked by other physicians.

Cleaning Wounds

There were some physicians, even in medieval times, who believed that cleaning wounds and keeping them covered and dry was important. Their ideas were generally disregarded, however. In the 1840s, some physicians began to look at what was happening in hospitals, particularly to women who had just given birth. They realized that infections were being transmitted by the physicians attending the women.

Timeline

1220 Hugh of Lucca recommends battlefield wounds be cleaned and sewn up to minimize infection

1843 Oliver Wendell Holmes publishes a paper suggesting that infections in women who had just given birth were transmitted by their physicians

1862 Louis Pasteur shows that bacteria, "germs," cannot self-generate in a closed environment, therefore they must come from outside

1867 Joseph Lister publishes the article *Antiseptic Principles of the Practice of Surgery,* which recommends using carbolic acid as an antiseptic

1865 Belgian chemist Jean Servais Stas devises the first modern tables of atomic weights using oxygen as a standard.

1866 Italian astronomer Giovanni Schiaparelli shows that meteor showers are associated with the orbits of comets.

1867 English surgeon Joseph Lister introduces phenol as a disinfectant in the hospital.

1867 Swedish chemist Alfred Nobel patents dynamite in Britain.

1865 1866 1867

In the United States, Oliver Wendell Holmes pleaded with medical authorities to make hospital wards cleaner places during the 1840s.

Cleaning Hands

The detailed research of Ignaz Semmelweiss in Austria showed that midwives who washed hands between treating patients transmitted less disease than physicians who did not wash their hands between patients. However, Semmelweiss's research was rejected by the medical establishment. Similarly, in the United States, Oliver Wendell Holmes also recognized that cleanliness was vital to prevent infections from spreading, but he, too, was ignored by the medical authorities.

Pasteur's Breakthrough

The breakthrough came in 1862. French chemist and microbiologist Louis Pasteur showed that human tissue kept in a sealed, sterilized, airtight place did not develop infections. But if it was in a sterilized place and still exposed to air, then the tissue became infected. In other words, the infection was being carried by tiny bacteria through the air, and did not come from the tissue itself.

TIMELINE
1868–1870

KEY:

- Biology and Medicine
- Engineering and Invention
- Astronomy and Math
- Chemistry and Physics

1868

1868 U.S. engineer George Westinghouse designs the air brake for steam locomotives.

1868 English astronomer William Huggins observes that the star Sirius is receding from Earth.

1869

1869 Swiss pathologist Johann Friedrich Miescher isolates deoxyribonucleic acid (DNA), which he calls "nuclein."

1869 Russian chemist Dmitri Mendeleyev compiles the first periodic table of the elements.

Antiseptics

Using the germ theory of disease, British physician Joseph Lister (1827–1912) recognized that it was essential to stop airborne germs infecting patients. His article *Antiseptic Principles of the Practice of Surgery* (1867) was a major breakthrough. In this, he recommended the use of carbolic acid (phenol) spray in operating theaters to reduce the chances of infection during surgery. Infection rates dropped dramatically and the benefits of antiseptics were undeniable.

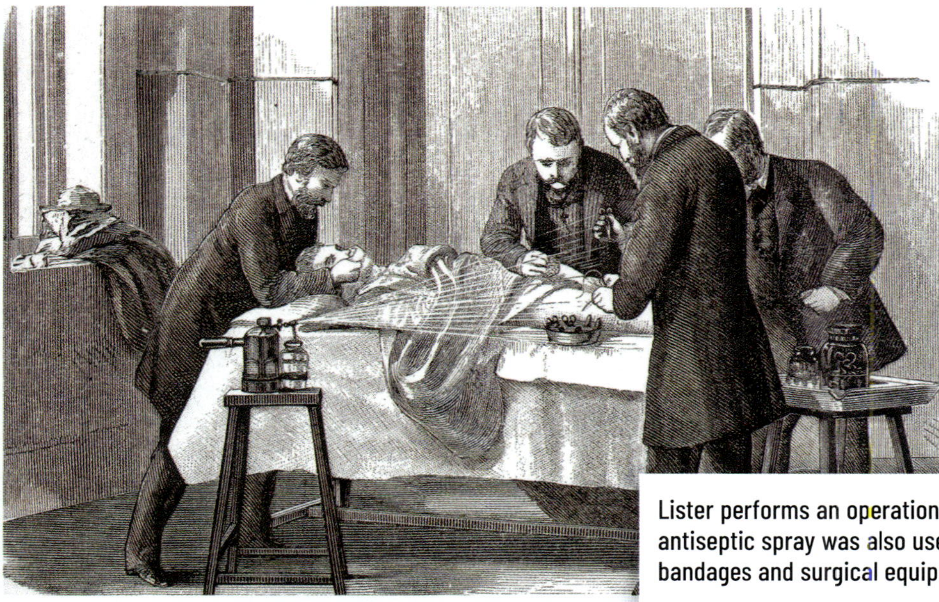

Lister performs an operation. His antiseptic spray was also used on bandages and surgical equipment.

1869 The Suez Canal between the Mediterranean Sea and Red Sea in Egypt is built by French engineer Ferdinand de Lesseps.

1869 The first transcontinental railroad, the Union Pacific, is completed.

1870 German chemist Rudolf Fittig makes aromatic hydrocarbons by combining two molecules of a halogen compound in the presence of sodium metal.

1870 German physicist Ernst Abbe introduces the use of his condenser to provide illumination for microscopes.

1869

1870

The Internal Combustion Engine

In the steam engines that powered the Industrial Revolution, external combustion took place. But the internal combustion engine was much more efficient.

German inventor Karl Benz (left) and his assistant ride on an 1885 Benz Motorwagen.

TIMELINE
1871–1873

KEY:

- Biology and Medicine
- Engineering and Invention
- Astronomy and Math
- Chemistry and Physics

1871

1871 German chemist Felix Hoppe-Seyler discovers invertase, the first enzyme to be isolated.

1871 U.S. engineer Simon Ingersoll invents a pneumatic rock drill.

1871 English inventor James Starley patents the "penny-farthing" bicycle.

The Belgian engineer Étienne Lenoir made the first successful engine to burn fuel internally in 1859. It ran on coal gas, which was mixed with air and sucked into the cylinder by the movement of a piston. The engine produced about 1 horsepower and worked in two jerky stages with the help of a heavy flywheel.

Timeline

1859 Gas-burning engine

1876 Four-stroke gas engine

1878 Two-stroke engine

1885 Gasoline engine

1892 Diesel engine

1929 Wankel engine

The First Engines

In 1862, French engineer Alphonse Beau de Rochas patented an engine that worked in four stages, or strokes. He did not build an actual engine, but the idea was later taken up by a self-taught German engineer, Nikolaus Otto. In 1876, Otto made his first horizontal four-stroke gas engine; it ran at about 180 rpm and produced 3 horsepower. The four-stroke cycle remains the basis of today's modern engines.

This German stamp celebrates Rudolf Diesel, who invented the diesel engine in 1892.

Otto's engine still used coal gas. In 1867, the Austrian engineer Siegfried Marcus invented a carburetor that vaporized liquid gasoline and mixed it with air. Two German engineers, Karl Benz and Gottlieb Daimler, independently made the first gasoline-burning internal combustion engines in 1885. Both engines were used to develop motor vehicles. Daimler's engine ran at 900 rpm and used a red-hot platinum tube to ignite the fuel and a

1872 The German mathematician Richard Dedekind publishes his theory of irrational numbers.

1872 Robert Chesebrough patents a version of petroleum jelly to soothe skin irritation. He markets it as Vaseline.

1873 Scottish physicist James Clerk Maxwell publishes his electromagnetic theory of light: that light is a form of electromagnetic radiation (like radio waves and X-rays).

1873 French engineer Amédée Bollée constructs a steam-powered car.

Two-Stroke Engine

In a two-stroke engine, the piston acts as a valve. On the upstroke, the piston compresses the fuel-and-air mixture, which is ignited by a spark from the spark plug. The piston closes off the exhaust port. The explosion forces the piston down (the downstroke). Exhaust gases escape via the uncovered port, and as the piston rises again, fresh fuel and air is sucked in through the open inlet port.

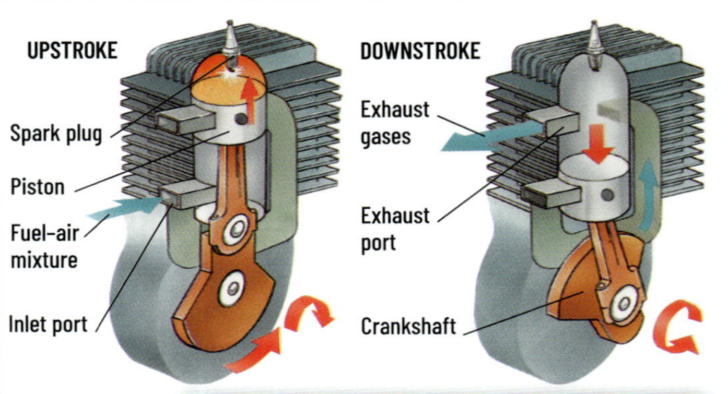

The up-and-down motion of the piston is turned into rotary motion by a crankshaft.

carburetor that had been invented by his business partner, German engineer Wilhelm Maybach. The engine built by Benz was slower than Daimler's (only 250 rpm) and produced less than 1 horsepower, but the car he used it in had many modern features, including coil ignition powered by a battery.

Improving Engines

By the end of the 19th century, the scientific principle of engines was being analyzed. If a suitable fuel–air mixture is hot and compressed enough, it will spontaneously combust. The Englishman Herbert Stuart patented the first example of a compression-ignition engine in 1890.

Two years later, a German inventor, Rudolf Diesel, patented a similar engine and demonstrated it in 1897. Since then, this type of engine has been known as a diesel engine. A diesel engine has several advantages. It uses a less refined,

TIMELINE

1874–1876

KEY:

- Biology and Medicine
- Engineering and Invention
- Astronomy and Math
- Chemistry and Physics

1874 U.S. physician Andrew Still founds osteopathy, which uses manipulation of bones and joints to treat diseases.

1874 Irish physicist George Stoney coins the phrase "electrine" for the fundamental unit of electricty; later he changes it to "electron."

1875 A safe loading level for ships, called the Plimsoll line, is introduced in Britain, and soon taken up everywhere.

1875 French physicist Jules Violle measures the solar constant—the amount of the sun's energy that reaches the top of Earth's atmosphere.

and therefore cheaper, fuel than gasoline. The engine needs no spark plugs or associated ignition system and is 35 percent efficient in fuel consumption, compared with 25 percent for the best gasoline engines. Both figures are far off the theoretical maximum efficiency of 67 percent for a perfect heat engine.

The early gasoline (and all diesel) engines were examples of reciprocating engines. There were some "rotary" gasoline engines, developed very successfully as power plants for propeller-driven aircraft.
In 1929, German engineer Felix Wankel patented a revolutionary internal combustion engine that was truly rotatory. The first prototype was made in 1956. A Wankel engine has a rotor that rotates inside a "cylinder" shaped like a fat figure eight.

Four-Stroke Engine

In a four-stroke engine, the inlet valve on the intake stroke opens as the piston moves down. This sucks a fuel-and-air mixture into the cylinder. On the compression stroke, the inlet valve closes and the piston rises, compressing the fuel and air. During the power stroke, the spark plug ignites the fuel, which explodes, and the hot gases force the piston down. On the fourth stroke, the exhaust valve opens to allow gases to escape while the piston rises.

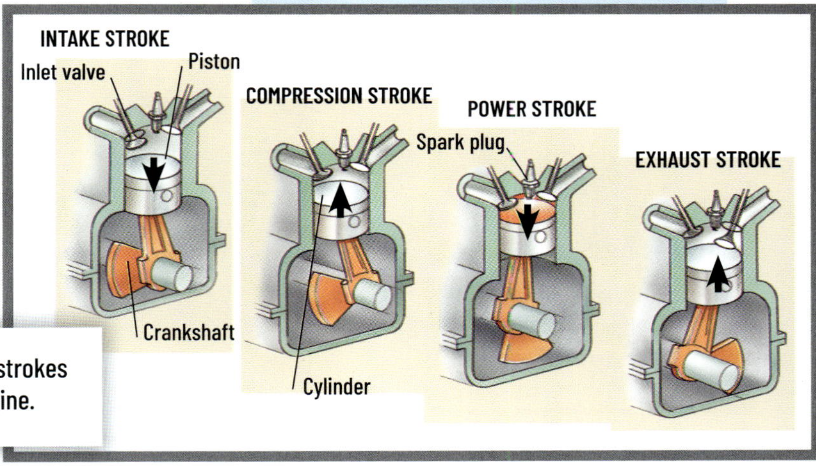

This diagram shows the four strokes of a standard four-stroke engine.

1876 German botanist Eduard Strasburger describes mitosis, the process of cell division into two identical cells.

1876 U.S. librarian Melvil Dewey introduces the Dewey Decimal System for cataloging library books.

1876

1876 Scottish-born U.S. engineer Alexander Graham Bell patents the telephone.

1876 German engineer Nikolaus Otto builds a four-stroke internal combustion engine fueled by coal gas.

Sources of Electricity

Before 1800, scientists knew only about static electricity—a positive or negative charge on an object—but then an Italian nobleman produced a moving electric current.

Volta shows off his battery, or voltaic pile, to Napoleon I, the emperor of France.

TIMELINE
1877–1880

KEY:
- Biology and Medicine
- Engineering and Invention
- Astronomy and Math
- Chemistry and Physics

1877

1877 German bacteriologist Robert Koch develops a way of staining bacteria to make them easier to study.

1877 Giovanni Schiaparelli, an Italian astronomer, reports that he has seen "canali" on the surface of Mars.

1878

1878 U.S. astronomer Asaph Hall discovers the two moons of Mars: Phobos and Deimos.

1878 U.S. inventor Thomas Alva Edison demonstrates his electric light bulb.

In 1791, Italian physician Luigi Galvani reported what he called "animal electricity." Dissecting a dead frog, he found the animal's muscles twitched when he touched them with two different metals. In 1800, Count Alessandro Volta, an Italian physicist, replaced the animal tissue with a cardboard disk soaked in salt solution. He put a piece of copper or silver on one side and zinc on the other side. Wires connected to the metal plates carried an electric current. Volta found he could obtain higher voltages by making a stack of such disks to form a voltaic battery (the first true battery).

Today, scientists call such a battery a primary cell. The pieces of metal are electrodes, and the solution between them is an electrolyte. In 1836, English chemist John Daniell produced a more efficient type of primary cell. Its current was steadier than Volta's cell and overcame the problem of polarization—a build-up of hydrogen bubbles on the copper electrode that eventually causes the voltaic pile to stop working.

Volta's Successors

The Leclanché cell, a battery invented in 1866 by French engineer Georges Leclanché, also avoids polarization. It uses an electrolyte of ammonium chloride solution. It produces about 1.5 volts. Today's common type of dry battery has the same system.

Timeline

1800 Voltaic pile

1836 Daniell cell

1859 Lead-acid accumulator

1866 Leclanché cell

1872 Clark standard cell

1893 Weston cadmium cell

1900 Nickel-iron accumulator

Luigi Galvani discovered that a frog's limbs twitched if he applied two types of metal to create an electric charge.

1879 English inventor Henry Lawson invents the "safety" bicycle, driven by a chain to the rear wheel—the model for all modern bicycles.

1880 French chemist Louis Pasteur identifies the Streptococcus bacterium.

1879

1880

1879 U.S. chemists discover saccharin, an artificial sweetener 2,000 times sweeter than sugar.

Primary Cell

A primary cell, such as the dry battery for a flashlight (below), can be used only until its chemicals run out, when it has to be thrown away (carefully). In this type of cell, the electrolyte is a paste of ammonium chloride and gum. The zinc cathode forms the case of the battery, and manganese dioxide and carbon surround the central carbon anode.

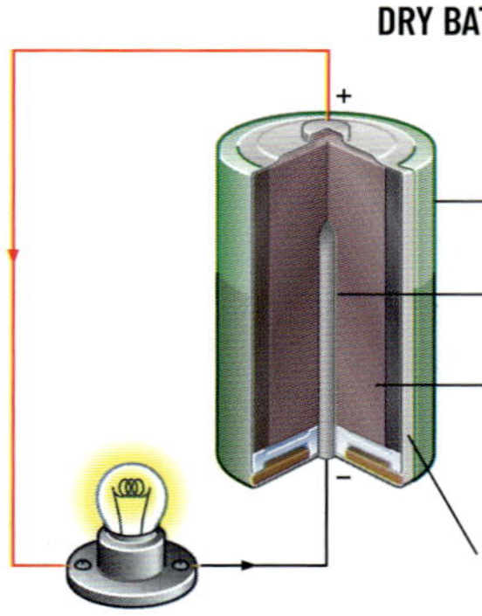

This battery uses carbon and zinc for the anode and cathode, respectively.

The Leclanché cell used the same principles as most modern dry batteries.

The German chemist Robert Bunsen made a zinc–carbon primary cell; using acid electrolytes, it produces 1.9 volts. The cadmium cell, invented in 1893 by English-born American electrical engineer Edward Weston, produces 1.0186 volts, and in 1908, the scientific community accepted it as a standard of voltage. It is known as the Weston standard cell. English electrical engineer Josiah Clark invented the Clark standard cell 21 years earlier, in 1872, using zinc instead of cadmium.

A primary cell stops working when it is fully discharged. A secondary cell (or storage cell, or accumulator) can be recharged. In 1859, French chemist Gaston Planté devised the lead–acid accumulator. It is the earliest and most commonly used battery, as used in most cars. It has one electrode (or "plate") of lead and one of lead covered with lead oxide, which dip into a sulfuric acid electrolyte. Another

TIMELINE
1880–1884

KEY:
Biology and Medicine
Engineering and Invention
Astronomy and Math
Chemistry and Physics

1880 Scottish astronomer George Forbes predicts the existence of "Planet X" orbiting beyond Neptune; Pluto is discovered in 1930.

1880 German bacteriologist Karl Eberth discovers the bacterium that causes typhoid fever.

1880

1881

1881 U.S. astronomer Henry Draper takes the first photographs of comets.

1881 English physicist J. J. Thompson predicts that an object's mass changes when it becomes electrically charged.

type, the alkaline nickel–iron accumulator, or Ni–Fe cell, was invented in 1900 by American inventor Thomas Edison. When any accumulator becomes discharged, it can be connected to a supply of DC (direct current) and recharged. For example, as a car's motor is running, the battery is continually recharged.

Both primary and secondary cells convert chemical energy into electrical energy. In doing so, they "consume" materials in the electrodes or electrolyte. A fuel cell, however, converts the chemical energy of a fuel directly into electrical energy. The first fuel cell, which "consumed" hydrogen and oxygen gases, was demonstrated in 1839 by the Welsh physicist and courtroom judge William Grove.

Secondary Cell

A secondary cell, or accumulator, can be recharged. It has lead and lead-oxide electrodes in a sulfuric acid electrolyte. In use, sulfate ions react with the lead cathode to produce lead sulfate and release electrons. To recharge the accumulator, current from an outside source is passed through the battery in the opposite direction. This reverses the reactions at the electrodes, reforming lead and lead oxide. The accumulator is then ready for use again.

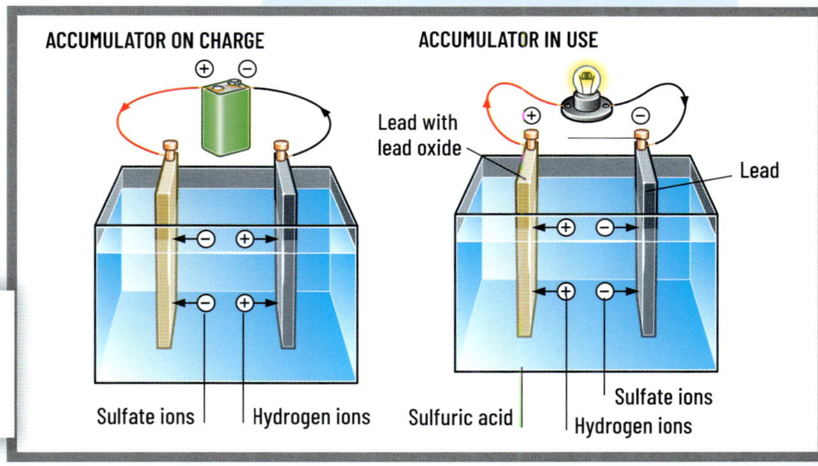

Car batteries are secondary cells, or accumulators, that are charged by the engine.

1882 German bacteriologist Robert Koch discovers the bacterium that causes tuberculosis and, in 1883, the bacterium that causes cholera.

1884 U.S.-born English inventor Hiram Maxim makes the first fully automatic machine gun.

1882 1883 1884

1882 The first U.S. steam-powered electricity-generating plant opens in New York City.

1883 Belgian engineer Étienne Lenoir invents the spark plug (for internal combustion engines).

Thomas Edison

Thomas Edison turned technological invention into a production line. He and his associates devised hundreds of devices that have defined the modern world.

It is often said of the 1800s that rather than any single invention being most important, the century invented the process of invention, so that inventions appeared in many areas of life. One important aspect of invention in the 1800s was that inventors could patent their new idea or product—no one else had the right to use it without the inventor's permission. Such patents had been granted earlier, by states such as Venice (as early as 1674), but in Britain, France, and the newly independent United States of America, patent legislation was not passed until the late 1700s. It protected inventors who were able to make money

Thomas Edison, the most prolific inventor of all time.

TIMELINE
1884–1885

KEY:

- Biology and Medicine
- Engineering and Invention
- Astronomy and Math
- Chemistry and Physics

1884 U.S. engineer Frank Sprague—"the father of electric railway traction"—forms the Sprague Electric Railway and Motor Company.

1884

1884 German physiologist Max Rubner shows that the body makes use of carbohydrates, fats, and proteins in order to produce energy.

1884 German astronomer Max Wolf discover's Wolf's comet, with a period of just seven years.

Thomas Edison with the second version of his phonograph.

Timeline

1869 Edison registers his first patent, for an electronic vote recorder

1876 Sells a multiplex telegraph patent and sets up his own laboratory

1877 Gains fame by patenting a phonograph, a device for reproducing sound

1880 Is granted a patent for an electric light bulb using a carbon filament

1891 Shows the public his kinetoscope, an early form of film technology

out of their creativity. The national patent offices quickly became important institutions of modern states, staffed by experts who decided whether an invention was worthy of being protected.

General Electric

Thomas Edison (1847–1931) worked as a telegraph operator and sold newspapers on railway platforms as a young man. He was fascinated by technology—

1885 Austrian doctor Sigmund Freud develops psychoanalysis as a diagnostic procedure.

1885 French chemist Louis Pasteur produces a vaccine against rabies.

1885

1885 U.S. architect William Jenney builds the world's first skyscraper, a steel-framed building in Chicago.

1885 U.S. electrical engineer William Stanley invents the transformer.

Thomas Edison's Menlo Park laboratory in New Jersey.

especially electrical technology. He was fired from one job because he ruined an office desk while using a battery with sulfuric acid during a nighttime experiment. Edison sold his invention of a new type of telegraphic apparatus in 1876. The proceeds helped him to fund a research unit in Menlo Park, New Jersey. There, he employed engineers and scientists who worked on projects under his supervision.

Edison was granted 1,093 patents. Ones that were particularly important were a phonograph that could reproduce sound, the incandescent electric light bulb, and the carbon microphone for use in telephony.

TIMELINE
1886–1890

KEY:

- Biology and Medicine
- Engineering and Invention
- Astronomy and Math
- Chemistry and Physics

1886 U.S. chemist John Pemberton invents Coca-Cola.

1887 German physicist Heinrich Hertz detects radio waves.

1888 Danish astronomer Johan Dreyer publishes a new catalog of nebulae and star clusters.

1886 1887 1888

Edison was also an astute businessman. He founded the Edison Electric Light Company in 1878, which grew into General Electric, one of the world's largest companies.

Edison's Legacy

Edison believed his ability to concentrate on new ideas was partly due to being extremely deaf, after suffering from scarlet fever as a child. During his lifetime he fought several court cases when other inventors claimed ownership of his inventions. His original mind and personal drive helped to bring about the technology in use across the world today.

The electric lighting of a modern city can be traced back to Edison's incandescent light bulb.

1889 The Eiffel Tower is completed in Paris, France.

1889 U.S. astronomer Edward Barnard takes the first photographs of the Milky Way (our galaxy).

1890 Ivan Pavlov begins experimenting with dogs to study how nerve impulses stimulate digestive secretion in the stomach.

1889 | 1889 | 1890

1889 Swedish physical chemist Svante Arrhenius derives the Arrhenius equation, a way of calculating the speed of a chemical reaction.

1890 U.S. inventor Herman Hollerith invents a punch-card reader (for recording census results).

1890 German bacteriologists produce antitoxins against the diseases diphtheria and tetanus.

The Elusive Electron

Today, every science student knows how important the electron is to our understanding of electricity and atomic physics. A century ago, things were very different.

J. J. Thomson won the Nobel Prize in Physics in 1906. Seven of his assistants were also awarded Nobel prizes.

TIMELINE
1891–1895

KEY:
- Biology and Medicine
- Engineering and Invention
- Astronomy and Math
- Chemistry and Physics

1891 German engineer Otto Lilienthal makes a steerable human-carrying glider.

1892 German bacteriologist Robert Koch introduces filtration of water to control a cholera epidemic in Hamburg, Germany.

1892 English scientist Francis Galton argues that no two people have the same fingerprints, and that fingerprints can be used in crime investigation.

Until the end of the 19th century, discoveries in physics had left unanswered questions such as: Objects can hold a charge of static electricity, but what form does the charge take? What are the electric current charges that flow along a conductor and are they different from the electrostatic ones? A high voltage across the plates of a vacuum tube produces cathode rays, but what are the rays made of? And if matter is made of atoms, what are atoms made of?

Timeline

1850 Geissler tubes invented

1874 Stoney predicts existence of electrons

1879 Crookes suggests cathode rays are particles

1891 Electron named

1895 Perrin proves cathode rays are made up of negative charges

1897 Electron discovered

The First Answers

The answer to these questions came from one invention—the vacuum pump. Scientists could now remove most of the air from any apparatus. Around 1850, the German laboratory equipment manufacturer Heinrich Geissler sealed metal plates inside a glass vacuum tube containing traces of a gas. He connected the plates to a source of high-voltage electricity and obtained pretty lighting effects as the gas glowed. Geissler tubes were used by two German physicists: Julius Plücker in 1859 and Johann Hittorf in 1869. They claimed the light resulted from "rays" traveling

This plaque marks the site of the Cavendish Laboratory in Cambridge, England.

1893 Black American surgeon Daniel Williams performs the first open-heart surgery.

1893 The French Lumière brothers invent a motion-picture camera.

1895 Swedish and Scottish chemists independently discover helium on Earth (previously it was only known in the sun's spectrum).

1893 1894 1895

1893 German engineer Rudolf Diesel first builds a compression-ignition engine (diesel engine).

1894 U.S. astronomer Percival Lowell sets up a private observatory at Flagstaff, Arizona, to search for the ninth planet.

1895 German physicist Wilhelm Röntgen takes the first X-ray.

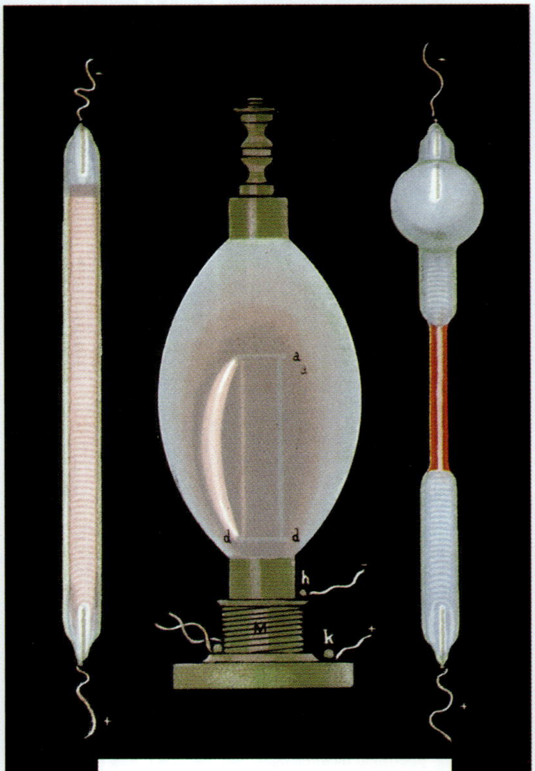

Geissler tubes are glass tubes or bulbs with most of the air pumped out of them.

in the Geissler tube. In 1879, English physicist William Crookes confirmed this and suggested the "rays" may be particles. Sixteen years later, French physicist Jean Perrin deflected these cathode rays.

Thomson and Cathode Rays

Then along came the English physicist J. J. Thomson. At age 14, he trained as a railroad engineer, then won a scholarship to Cambridge University, graduating in 1880. He worked in the Cavendish Laboratory, and became head of the laboratory in 1884.

Thomson deflected cathode rays with electric and magnetic fields, measured their speed (proving they travel more slowly than light waves), and figured out the ratio of their charge (e) to their mass (m). Thomson deduced that cathode rays must consist of minute negatively charged particles. He announced the discovery of the first subatomic particles in 1897, and in 1899 found they have a mass equal to about one two-thousandth of the mass of a hydrogen atom. In 1874, George Stoney had predicted their existence, and in 1891, he named them "electrons." The electron was the unit of electricity responsible for electrostatic charges. It became clear that a flow of electrons along a

TIMELINE
1895–1900

KEY:

- Biology and Medicine
- Engineering and Invention
- Chemistry and Physics

1895

1895 King Gillette has the idea for the disposable double-edge razor blade.

1896

1896 French physicist Henri Becquerel discovers radioactivity.

1896 New Zealand-born British physicist Ernest Rutherford describes and names alpha particles (which are helium nuclei) and beta particles (which are electrons).

1897

1897 German physicist Ferdinand Braun invents the cathode-ray tube, later used in TV sets.

1897 Physicist J. J. Thompson identifies the electron, the first subatomic particle.

conductor was an electric current. Since electrons come from the metal of the cathode, they must be part of all atoms.

J. J. Thomson studied canal rays, which led in 1912 to a way of separating charged particles. In 1919, the English physicist Francis Aston developed the mass spectograph. When Thomson retired in 1919, he was succeeded by his former assistant, Ernest Rutherford. Rutherford eventually proposed a structure for the atom that included the atomic nucleus.

Electricity Flow

Electrons occur in all atoms. In most metals—such as the copper in electric cable—many electrons leave their atoms to form a "sea" of free electrons (bottom of diagram). When a voltage is applied (middle section), the free electrons move to form an electric current. Copper is said to have low resistance. A metal with high resistance, such as tungsten used in electric heaters, has few free electrons (top section). A voltage causes only a small current, and the metal becomes hot.

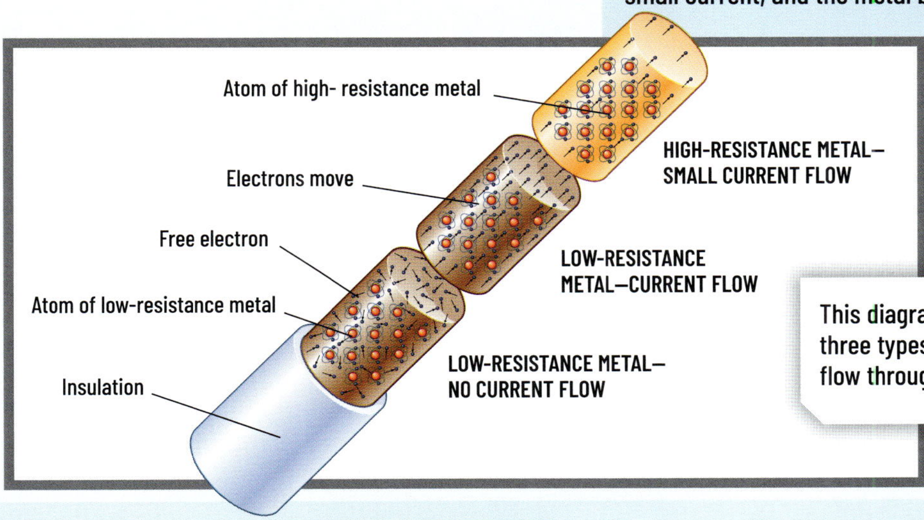

This diagram shows three types of electrical flow through a cable.

1898 English physician Ronald Ross finds the microorganism plasmodia, which causes malaria, in the stomach of a mosquito; he argues that mosquito bites transfer the parasite to humans.

1898 English physiologist John Langley identifies the autonomic nervous system, which controls involuntary muscles and glands.

1898 French chemists Pierre and Marie Curie discover the elements polonium and radium.

1898

1900

1900 Austrian-born U.S. pathologist Karl Landsteiner discovers the A, B, and O blood groups and their intercompatability.

1900 German physicist Max Planck proposes the quantum theory: that radiation is emitted in separate "packets," or quanta.

Glossary

absolute zero The lowest temperature possible (equal to –459.67°F/–273.15°C).

atom The smallest unit that matter can be divided into and still retain its chemical identity.

bacteria (Singular bacterium) Microscopic organisms that can cause disease.

chromosome A threadlike structure in the nucleus of a living cell that carries the genetic information.

compound, chemical A substance in which molecules are made up from atoms of more than one element.

conductor Any substance that allows an electric current, heat, or sound to pass through it.

ecology The study of the relationship of plants and animals to their environment and to each other.

electric current A flow of electrons through a conductor.

electromagnetism The phenomenon by which magnetic fields can be produced by the flow of electrons in an electronic current.

electron A negatively charged subatomic particle.

element Any substance that cannot be split chemically into simpler substances.

gene The basic unit of inheritance that controls a characteristic of an organism.

geology The group of sciences concerned with the study of Earth, including its structure, long-term history, composition, and origins.

microorganism The general term for any living organism that is invisible to the naked eye but visible under a microscope.

photosynthesis The process by which green plants convert light energy from the sun.

subatomic particle Any particle that is smaller than an atom.

vaccine A preparation containing viruses or other microorganisms introduced into the body to build up immunity against infectious disease.

virus A tiny parasitic organism that can reproduce only inside the cell of its host.

Further Information

Books

Dorling Kindersley. *How Technology Works: The Facts Visually Explained*. Dorling Kindersley, 2019.

Bayarri, Jordi. *Louis Pasteur and the Power of Observation* (Graphic Science Biographies). Lerner Publishing Group, 2023.

Newland, Sonya. *Extraordinary Bridges: The Science of How and Why They Were Built.* Capstone Publishing, 2019.

Rogers, Kate. *From 1860 to 1920—Louis Pasteur to Henrietta Swan Leavitt* (History's Most Influential Scientists). Rosen Publishing, 2024.

Woods, Michael and Mary B. Woods. *Machines Through the Ages. From Furnaces to Factories* (Technology Through the Ages). Lerner Publishing Group, 2024.

Websites

www.amnh.org/exhibitions/darwin
The American Museum of Natural History's page on Darwin's life and works, with other pages on his voyages with illustrations and diagrams.

www.history.com/topics/inventions/thomas-edison
History.com pages on Thomas Edison, with videos and numerous link to his inventions.

www.sciencemuseum.org.uk/objects-and-stories/medicine/listers-antisepsis-system.
Pages and links on Joseph Lister and antiseptic systems and surgery.

www.thoughtco.com/history-of-electricity-1989860
Thoughtco.com's page on the history of electricity, with many links.

Index